DATE DUE

Margery Facklam

What's the Buzz?

The Secret Lives of Bees

RAINTREE
STECK-VAUGHN
PUBLISHERS

A Harcourt Company

Austin · New York
www.steck-vaughn.com

To all kids who love to know about bees

Steck-Vaughn Company

Copyright © 2001 Turnstone Publishing Group.
Copyright © 2001, text, by Margery Facklam.

First published 2001 by Raintree Steck-Vaughn Publishers, an imprint of Steck-Vaughn Company.

Library of Congress Cataloging-in-Publication Data

Facklam, Margery.
    What's the buzz?: the secret lives of bees / Margery Facklam.
    p. cm.—(Turnstone rain forest pilot book)
    Includes bibliographical references (p.).
        ISBN 0-7398-2219-5 (hardcover)   ISBN 0-7398-2228-4 (softcover)
        1. Bees—Behavior—Juvenile literature. [1. Bees.] I. Title. II. Series.
    QL565.2 .F33 2000   00-033284
    595.79'9—dc21

For information about this and other Turnstone reference books and educational materials, visit Turnstone Publishing Group on the World Wide Web at http://www.turnstonepub.com.

Photo and illustration credits listed on page 48 constitute part of this copyright page.

Printed and bound in the United States of America

1 2 3 4 5 6 7 8 9 0 LB 05 04 03 02 01 00

Contents

1 What's the Buzz?

Day-active
sweat bee

European
honeybee

Nocturnal
sweat bee

Africanized
honeybee

Stingless
bee

There are many kinds of bees, and most don't look alike. Bees come in just about every color of the rainbow. They range in size from 2 mm to 4 cm (.08 to 1.6 inches). These drawings are a little more than three times larger than life.

"**W**hat do bees do?" Ask most people and they will say, "Bees make honey and they sting." They may even tell you that bees are fuzzy, black-and-yellow insects that live in hives. But there are lots of kinds of bees, and they're not all the same. Some fly at night. Some can't sting. Some live only a few months, and others live several years. Every species of bee has its own story. A species is one of the groups used by scientists to classify, or group, living things. Animals of the same species can mate with each other. And they give birth to young that can mate and give birth, or reproduce.

Scientists have named about 20,000 species of bees. But they think there may be as many as 40,000 species. Why so many?

Over millions of years, environments change. Animals slowly evolve, or change, too. These changes help the animals survive, or live, so that they can reproduce. And it's reproducing that matters, not how long an animal lives.

To survive, some bee species developed new ways to live together. Some found new ways to "talk" to each other, or communicate. Others

4

developed other new skills and new behaviors. Scientists call these kinds of changes adaptations. Over a long time, a group of bees can change so much it becomes a new species.

Bees come in different sizes. There are fat bumblebees and bees not much bigger than the tip of a pencil. There are bees of many colors, from dull black to glittering green. Some species of tropical bees are such bright reds and blues that they sparkle in the sun like little jewels.

Most bees play an important role in plant reproduction. Bees collect pollen, a powderlike material that flowers make. By carrying pollen from one flower to another, bees help plants reproduce. Bees are among the world's most important insects. Without them, many plants might not survive. And for most animals, life would be impossible without plants.

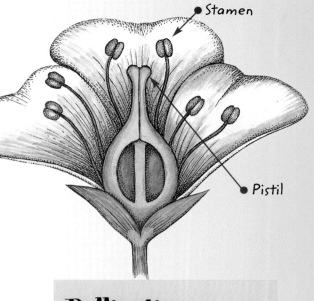

Stamen

Pistil

Pollination

Pollination is the first step in making seeds. The male part of the plant is called the stamen. The female part is called the pistil. A plant can't make seeds until the pollen from the stamen reaches the pistil. Some flowers pollinate themselves when pollen from the stamen falls on the pistil. Other flowers are pollinated when pollen blows from one flower to another.

Many animals spread pollen. But bees are the best pollinators of all. They go to flowers to gather pollen for food. Bees collect pollen in different ways. Some bees gather pollen from flower stamens by brushing against them. Some of the pollen then rubs off on the next flower the bees visit. In this way, bees spread pollen from flower to flower as they gather food.

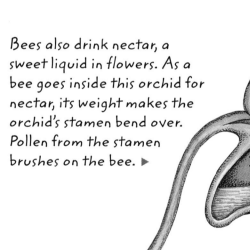

Bees also drink nectar, a sweet liquid in flowers. As a bee goes inside this orchid for nectar, its weight makes the orchid's stamen bend over. Pollen from the stamen brushes on the bee. ▶

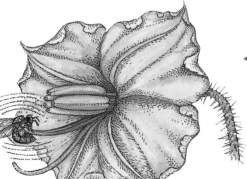

◀ Stingless bees like this one sometimes shake themselves to gather pollen from flowers. Shaking loosens the pollen and makes it fall on the bee.

What Is a Bee?

How do scientists know if an insect they see is a bee? Bees can be different sizes, shapes, or colors, but there are some things almost all bees have in common. First, all adult bees have two pairs of wings and six legs. The wings are usually clear in color. Most bees are hairy. They have special hairs on their abdomen or hind legs that they use to carry pollen. Most bees feed pollen and honey to their young.

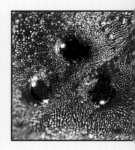

Compound Eyes •
These are large eyes made of many tiny lenses. Honeybee eyes like this one are hairy.

• Ocelli
These small eyes are used to find the horizon.

Antenna •
Bees communicate by smelling other bees with the tips of their antennae.

Forewing •
The wings of each bee species have their own vein patterns.

Hindwing •
The hindwings are connected to the forewings by a set of small hooks. The hooks keep the wings beating at the same time.

The hairs on a bee leg branch out. This is one way to tell a bee from other insects.

Legs •
Bees use their front and middle legs for cleaning. The middle legs also transfer pollen from the back legs.

This is an artist's picture of a *Lasioglossum microlepoides* bee. Its color is a shiny black-green.

Head
The head holds the bee's mouth parts, eyes, antennae, and brain.

Thorax
The thorax holds the muscles that power the bee's legs and wings.

Abdomen
The abdomen holds the bee's digestive and reproductive parts.

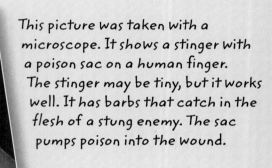

This picture was taken with a microscope. It shows a stinger with a poison sac on a human finger. The stinger may be tiny, but it works well. It has barbs that catch in the flesh of a stung enemy. The sac pumps poison into the wound.

Bees, such as this bumblebee, use their mandibles, or jaws, for many purposes. Bees use them to eat, feed their young and the queen, build nests, and even fight.

This honeybee is heading home after collecting pollen. Bees have hairy areas on their hind legs to which pollen sticks. Bees can pack large bundles of pollen onto their legs and still fly.

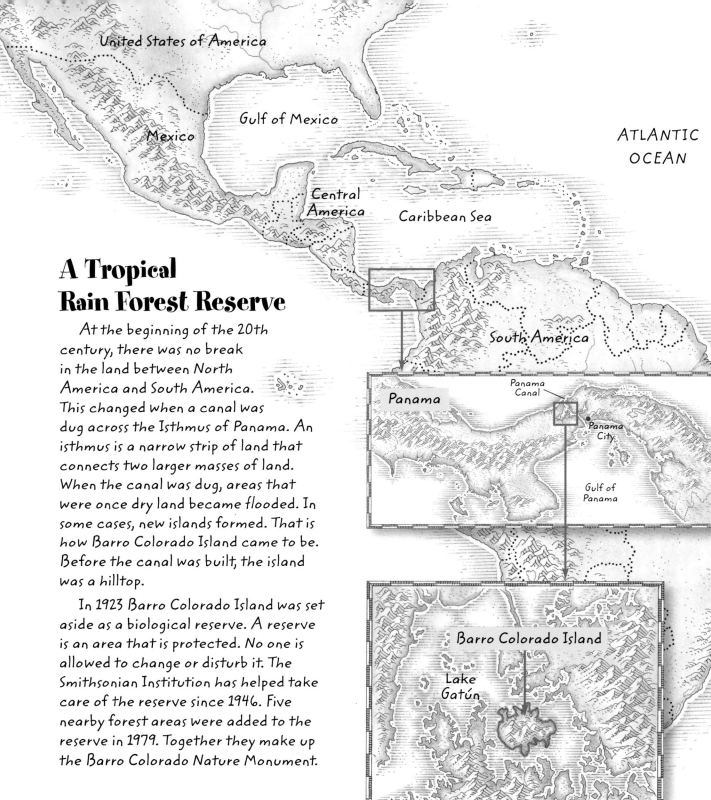

United States of America

Gulf of Mexico

Mexico

Central America

Caribbean Sea

ATLANTIC OCEAN

South America

A Tropical Rain Forest Reserve

At the beginning of the 20th century, there was no break in the land between North America and South America. This changed when a canal was dug across the Isthmus of Panama. An isthmus is a narrow strip of land that connects two larger masses of land. When the canal was dug, areas that were once dry land became flooded. In some cases, new islands formed. That is how Barro Colorado Island came to be. Before the canal was built, the island was a hilltop.

In 1923 Barro Colorado Island was set aside as a biological reserve. A reserve is an area that is protected. No one is allowed to change or disturb it. The Smithsonian Institution has helped take care of the reserve since 1946. Five nearby forest areas were added to the reserve in 1979. Together they make up the Barro Colorado Nature Monument.

Panama

Panama Canal

Panama City

Gulf of Panama

Barro Colorado Island

Lake Gatún

N

PACIFIC OCEAN

8

Stingless Bees

David Roubik is a scientist at the Smithsonian Tropical Research Institute (STRI) in Panama City, Panama. He also conducts experiments on nearby Barro Colorado Island. For more than 20 years, David has studied bees in tropical forests.

David is an expert on the many species of bees called stingless bees. They live only in the tropics, just to the north and south of Earth's equator. These bees can't sting, but they can bite. Thousands of stingless bees can live together in one nest with a queen bee that lays most of the eggs.

Female bees, called workers, feed and care for the queen. Workers build and guard the nest, and gather the food. The males, called drones, leave home and try to mate with a queen at another nest. That's their only job.

Worker bees build a nest by making small rooms called cells. Stingless bees use wax or wax mixed with tree sap to make these cells. Below is a picture of workers from the *Melipona interrupta grandis* species of stingless bees. They are in a nest inside a hollow tree branch.

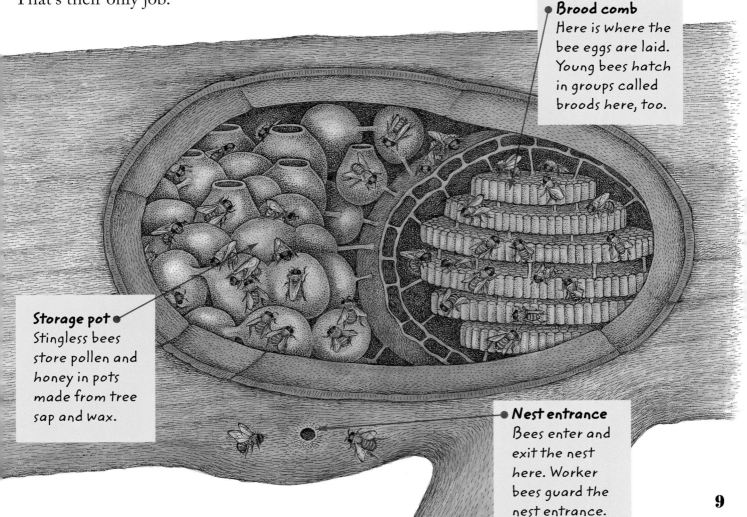

Brood comb
Here is where the bee eggs are laid. Young bees hatch in groups called broods here, too.

Storage pot
Stingless bees store pollen and honey in pots made from tree sap and wax.

Nest entrance
Bees enter and exit the nest here. Worker bees guard the nest entrance.

This stingless bee forager found a good source of food. It went back to the nest and told the other bees where to find the flower.

The female workers who look for food are called foragers. They collect pollen and nectar, a liquid that flowers make. In a rain forest, such as the one on Barro Colorado Island, many different species of bees look for pollen and nectar. Butterflies and other insects gather this food, too. All of these animals compete to find and collect food.

But stingless bees have an adaptation that gives them an advantage. They can tell other workers where to find food. How does an insect with a brain smaller than a grass seed do this?

That's what David and fellow scientist James Nieh wanted to find out. "In the rain forest, there are about a thousand different species of flowering plants the bees can go to," David says. "Bees go out, maybe as far as two or three kilometers (about one or two miles), and bring back food. And they tell each other exactly where to go." How do they do this?

What happened then? The bees in the nest got the message. They followed the stingless bee forager's directions to the food.

Finding the Flowers

James and David came up with an experiment to learn how stingless bees communicate. They based their work on studies that scientist Karl von Frisch did in the 1930s. Von Frisch discovered how honeybees give directions. They do a "waggle dance." They waggle their bodies to direct other bees to food.

David and James studied stingless bees, which are relatives of honeybees. Stingless bees don't do a waggle dance, so how do they communicate directions?

As James and David studied these bees, they discovered more about the bees' language. "Finding out how well the bees communicate really shocked us," David says. "They're not just saying that there's some good food out there, so fly around and maybe you'll find it. They're saying how far away, how high up, and in what direction."

David and James set up experiments to study how the stingless bee foragers tell recruits where to find food. A recruit is a worker bee that joins the foragers. David and James put a colony, or group, of stingless bees into a wooden nest inside their laboratory. The nest has a glass window.

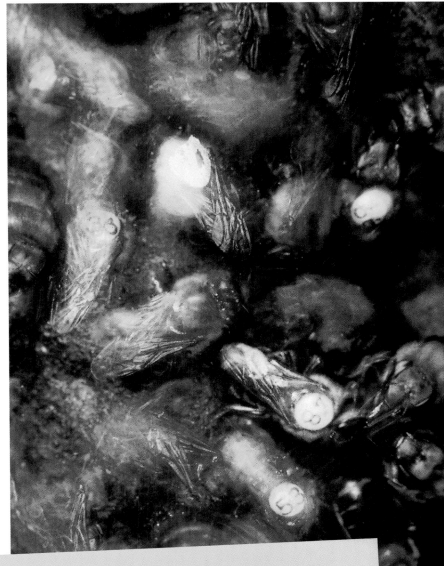

Waggle Dancing

Honeybees tell each other where to find food by doing a waggle dance. A dancing forager uses the sun to tell other bees where the food is. For example, if the food is in the same direction as the sun, the bee dances with its head pointed up from the ground. If the food is in the opposite direction, the bee dances with its head pointed down.

Bees always seem to know where the sun is, even when it's cloudy outside or when they are inside the nest. Some bees dance for up to half an hour in the nest. These bees change their head position to match the movement of the sun. Bees can keep track of the sun's position even when they can't see it.

A Home in the Laboratory

◄ David and James wanted to know more about what bees do in their nests. To find out, they set up this bee nest inside their laboratory. A camera films the inside of the nest. The nest's entrance is the hole under the watch. The watch is there to show the time when something happens. The yellow and black centimeter marks show the size of each bee.

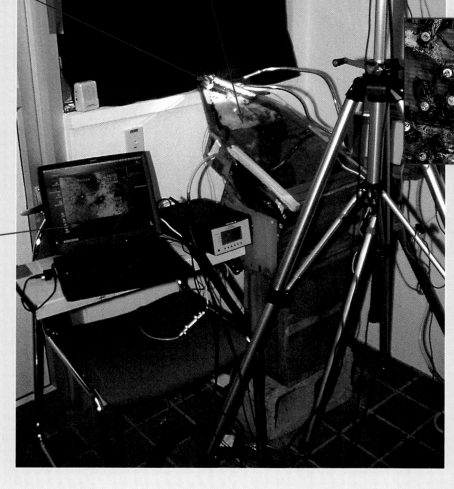

● A video camera films bees inside the nest.

This is the tube that connects the nest to the outside. ●

The video camera is hooked up to a computer. Right now the computer shows a close-up of two bees that have just come into the nest. ●

▲ This is the nest entrance, seen from outside the laboratory. It is built to look like a natural nest entrance.

It also has an opening to the outside that lets the bees come and go. That way, the scientists can see what the bees are doing. They can see foragers leave the nest. They can watch the foragers return with food and tell other workers where to find it.

But all the worker bees look alike. How do David and James know which bees are foragers and which are recruits? They paint each forager with a different colored dot. Or they glue a number onto the bee's back with a mild glue.

(above)
As each bee eats in a feeder, a scientist adds a dot of bright color or glues a number to its back. This helps scientists keep track of the bees.

(below)
James keeps track of the different paint colors in his logbook.

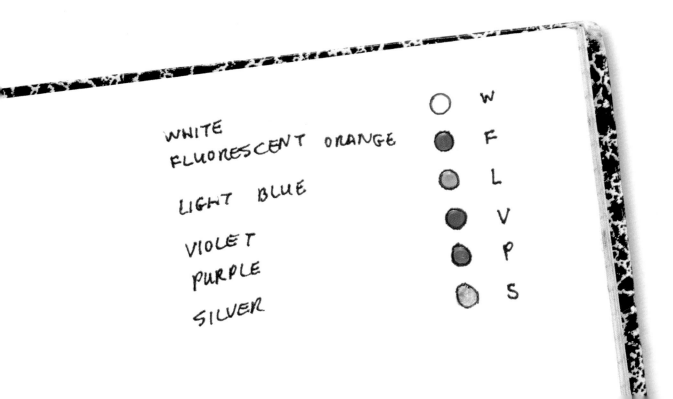

WHITE   ○   W
FLUORESCENT ORANGE   ●   F
LIGHT BLUE   ●   L
VIOLET   ●   V
PURPLE   ●   P
SILVER   ●   S

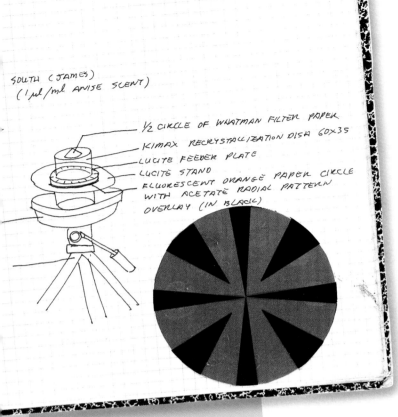

SOUTH (JAMES)
(1 μl/ml ANISE SCENT)

½ CIRCLE OF WHATMAN FILTER PAPER
KIMAX RECRYSTALLIZATION DISH 60X35
LUCITE FEEDER PLATE
LUCITE STAND
FLUORESCENT ORANGE PAPER CIRCLE
WITH ACETATE RADIAL PATTERN
OVERLAY (IN BLACK)

(above)
James' logbook shows a diagram of how he built the feeder. That way, if this feeder works well, he can make others just like it.

(below)
Here the first foragers in the experiment leave the laboratory nest.

To do the experiment, David and James trained forager bees to go to a feeder. First, they filled the feeder with sugar water that tasted like nectar. To get the bees' attention, they squirted sugar water into the bees' nest. Then, they put the feeder close to the nest entrance. Once the bees had a good drink, James and David slowly moved the feeder away from the nest. As long as the feeder wasn't moved too fast or too far away, the bees could find it.

The idea was to make sure each forager tasted the nectar in the feeder. The foragers would then fly back to the nest and tell recruits where to find this new food.

The recruits found the feeder. But how could David and James be sure that the recruits were getting directions from the foragers? The scientists set up a second feeder that was just like the first one. This was the control. A control is a copy of an experiment, with one difference. Here the difference was that the bees were not trained to go to the control feeder. If recruits went to the first feeder and not to the control feeder, the scientists would know that the recruits were following the foragers' directions.

For the first part of the experiment, David and James trained the bees to go to a feeder north of the nest. They put the control feeder the same distance from the nest, but to the south. James watched one feeder and David watched the other. They wrote down each bee's number at each feeder. They thought that if the trained foragers went back to the nest and gave directions to recruits, the recruits would go to the north feeder. And that's what

In this photograph the foragers have found the first feeder. Andy Torres films them so that James and David can study their behavior later.

happened. The recruits got the message and most of them flew to the north feeder. They didn't go to the south feeder because they didn't get directions to go there. This part of the experiment showed that the bees could communicate direction.

Could the foraging bees tell recruits how far away the food was? The scientists tested the foraging bees again. This time they put the feeders at different distances to see if the bees could communicate distance. They could. Most recruits went to the feeder the foragers told them about.

Here James is at the top of the tower with the first feeder. David is at the bottom of the tower with a control feeder.

Follow the Leader?

But what if the recruits were just following the foragers? To be sure that wasn't happening, David and James did the experiment again. This time James captured all the bees in plastic bags as they left the nest. He kept the foragers that had been to the feeder. Then, he let the recruits go. The recruits found the correct feeder. This proved that they weren't just following the foragers.

Now David and James had another question. Could foragers tell recruits to fly up to a certain height? That's important in a rain forest. Many flowers are far above the ground in the canopy. The canopy is where the treetops cross over each other to form a ceiling of leaves. For this experiment, James carried the first feeder to the top of a metal tower 40 meters (about 130 feet) high. David watched the control feeder on the ground.

The scientists thought that if the foragers told

16

the other bees how high the food was, then almost no recruits would go to the feeder on the ground. They would go straight to the one at the top of the tower. And that's what they did. The stingless bees could communicate height.

Could they communicate through smell? Some stingless bee species put drops of liquid on leaves. The drops have a scent, or smell. Were the recruits following a scent trail? To find out, David and James put the first feeder in a canoe and paddled it across a bay. They knew that foragers couldn't leave a scent trail on water. If recruits were going to find this feeder, they would have to follow directions. Again, most recruits flew straight to the feeder on the other side of the water. They went where the foragers told them to go.

The foragers gave the recruits messages about distance, direction, and height. But how?

The research station where David and James work is on Barro Colorado Island on Lake Gatún. David and James used the lake in their experiments. They found that foragers could tell recruits how to find food, even when the food was on the other side of the lake.

17

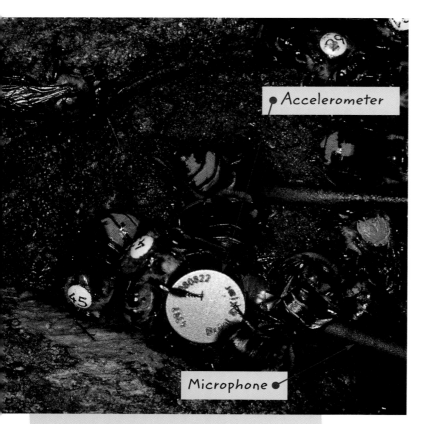

Accelerometer

Microphone

Bee Sentences

David and James looked at films of foragers returning to the laboratory nest. When a forager returns to the nest from a good food source, she buzzes loudly while she unloads her food. The scientists used the films to compare the buzzing of bees from different feeders.

James and David found out that when foragers buzz while unloading food, they are telling how high off the ground the food is. Long buzzes mean the food is near the ground. Short buzzes mean the food is higher. After unloading food, foragers dance by spinning clockwise or counterclockwise. As they dance, they buzz to tell distance. The shorter the buzzes, the closer the food. The longer the buzzes, the farther away the food is.

David and James used a computer to make pictures of the bee sounds. The pictures were then printed on strips of paper so that David and James could measure the bees' sounds more accurately.

They also are comparing stingless bees with other bees that don't have a language. They want to understand how language helps animals survive and compete. One thing they want to know, for example, is what recruits listen to. Do they pay attention to the foragers' buzzing sounds? Or do they feel vibrations through their feet when the foragers buzz? "We have a lot more to learn about these bees. Many new experiments are being planned for the future," James says. What David and James discover in their experiments will help other scientists, too.

(above)
James uses a microphone and an accelerometer to study bees. The microphone records bees' sounds. The accelerometer records vibrations. The bees in this experiment are marked with numbers rather than colors.

(below)
Two small lights help James and David study bees that live outside the laboratory. These bees live in a nearby tree. The lights help the scientists see what's happening at the nest entrance. The letters "COL C" on the tree stand for Colony C, the scientists' name for this nest of bees.

Picture This!

Here's a picture of bee sounds. This kind of picture is called an oscillogram. An oscillogram shows how long a sound lasts and how loud it is. On an oscillogram, louder sounds have higher amplitudes. The amplitude is the distance between the center line and the top or bottom of each shape in the picture.

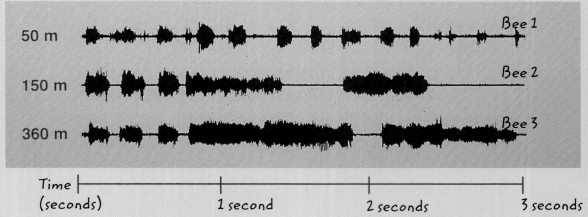

Bee Sounds Communicating Distance

Distance from the nest (meters)

50 m — Bee 1

150 m — Bee 2

360 m — Bee 3

Time (seconds) | 1 second | 2 seconds | 3 seconds

This oscillogram shows the sounds that three different bees made while they danced. The pictures vary depending on how far the bees went to find food. Bee 1 traveled 50 meters (about 160 feet). It made short bursts of sound that are fairly evenly spaced. Bee 3 traveled 360 meters (about 1,200 feet). It made three short sounds followed by two long sounds.

The oscillogram shows sounds that the bees made in a little more than two seconds. People could never hear the differences in these sounds. Comparing sound pictures like these helps James and David understand how the bees communicate distance.

2 Bee Lifestyles

This sweat bee is coming out of its home, an underground tunnel. Some sweat bee tunnels are short, no more than 5 centimeters (about 2 inches). Other tunnels are as long as 180 centimeters (about 6 feet).

If you've ever had a bee land on your arm and lick the perspiration, you've met a sweat bee. They seem to like the taste of salt. There are more than 5,000 species of sweat bees. And different sweat bees live in different ways. Some sweat bees are solitary, meaning they live alone. Others are social and live in groups. Their groups are called societies.

All male sweat bees are solitary. Female sweat bees can choose to be either solitary or social. If they are social, they live with other females. Most sweat bee nests are started by a queen bee, a single female. Queens that become social bees usually live with their daughters.

There are different kinds of sweat bee societies. One kind of society is called a communal nest. In this kind of society, every bee helps dig the nest and collect food. And every female bee reproduces.

In other sweat bee societies, the queen lays most of the eggs. The other bees dig tunnels, collect food, and guard the nest. Sometimes they fight over which one gets food or the best space to lay eggs.

Differences in societies interest scientists. If reproducing is the most important thing for animals, why do some bees create a society where only one animal, the queen, reproduces? It's a very big change that happened over a long time. How did it happen? And why? Scientists don't know. These are the kinds of questions scientist Bill Wcislo at STRI is interested in answering.

Bill Wcislo looks for sweat bee nests in flat, open places with some bare earth. He also looks in the banks of streams. Nests can be in backyards, gardens, empty lots, and wherever there are flowers and bare ground.

Home Sweet Home

Some sweat bees live in hollow twigs or vines. But most of them live in the ground. They dig tunnels that go almost straight down. One or more tunnels branch away from the main tunnel. The nests are often dug into banks along creeks and streams.

Off the sides of the main tunnel, the bees build or dig small cells. One larva, or baby bee, will live in each cell. Before they lay their eggs, the female bees paint the cell walls with chemicals that their bodies make.

"We think these chemicals help keep the right conditions, such as humidity, or moistness, for the larvae," Bill says. The chemicals also may help keep the cell clean and free from disease.

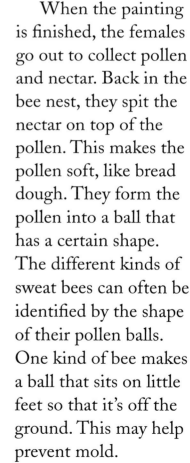

When the painting is finished, the females go out to collect pollen and nectar. Back in the bee nest, they spit the nectar on top of the pollen. This makes the pollen soft, like bread dough. They form the pollen into a ball that has a certain shape. The different kinds of sweat bees can often be identified by the shape of their pollen balls. One kind of bee makes a ball that sits on little feet so that it's off the ground. This may help prevent mold.

(above)
This is a *Dieunomia heteropoda* bee egg inside a cell. The egg has been laid on top of a golden-colored pollen ball.

(below)
After an egg hatches, it becomes a larva. The larva uses the pollen ball for food. The bee will stay in the cell until it's fully grown.

A female lays one egg on top of each pollen ball. Then, she closes the cells with a little dirt. The eggs hatch into larvae that eat the pollen balls. But the cells stay closed until the bees become adults. "It's like having a child and locking it in a bedroom with a supply of food until the child is full grown," Bill says.

It may take a day or more for a bee to collect enough food for one cell. But some female sweat bees cheat. They sneak into the nests of other females and lay their eggs on pollen they didn't collect. A bee that does this is called a parasite. A parasite is an animal or plant that lives off another living thing, which is called a host.

This growing bee is at the pupa stage. A pupa is in the stage of development between larva and adult.

Some bees behave as parasites only at certain times. But others have to be parasites. They don't know how to make nests or collect pollen anymore. Over time, they even lose the body parts for pollen collecting and nest making. They have no choice but to use the nests and food of other sweat bees.

Comparing the behavior of parasites and social bees helps scientists understand how animals can change their environments. It also helps them understand how changing environments can slowly shape animal behavior and body parts.

On the Ground and in the Trees

Bill used the comparative method to help him find out why there are bee nests both on the ground and in the trees. He gathered information from 90 different species of bees and wasps.

Bill compared the number of dead young in each nest. He found that ground nesters like the bee in the big picture below were attacked more often. So nesting in trees might help keep bees safe.

The Comparative Method

Bill wonders how the lives of bees have evolved over millions and millions of years. To find answers, he looks at the social behavior of bees. Bill compares the behaviors of different populations. A bee population is all the bees of the same species that live in a particular place, or environment. If two populations behave differently from each other, it is probably because they live in different environments.

Bill also collects information on different species of sweat bees. He then compares bee behavior with the behavior of other animals that live in societies, including humans.

This way of studying animals is called the comparative method. Comparisons help scientists understand the way changing environments cause changes in animal societies. Using the comparative method also helps scientists understand the advantages of different ways of life.

Digging for Answers

Bill wants to understand how sweat bees live together. To do this, he collects samples from many nests. Then, he compares the ways different sweat bees behave.

Bill goes out at least once a week and squirts water and plaster into a sweat bee tunnel. The plaster hardens as it dries. Then, Bill digs out the hardened plaster with his pocket knife. The plaster traps adult bees that he can study. It also helps him find cells that hold larvae and pupae.

Bill explains, "When we're digging out these tunnels, we also make notes about the weather, temperature, and how much pollen there is in the area." These notes are important because weather, temperature, and food supply may affect bee behavior.

For example, in some places the summer is short, and flowers bloom for only a short time. A female sweat bee who lives in that environment may not live long enough to have more than one brood, or group of young. So there can't be a social colony made of a mother and her daughters. For a social colony like this to develop, there must be time for a mother bee to have at least two broods of bees during a summer.

Bill digs out hardened plaster from sweat bee tunnels so that he can study the bees inside. Some of the tunnels have branches with places for cells. Others go straight into the ground with no branches.

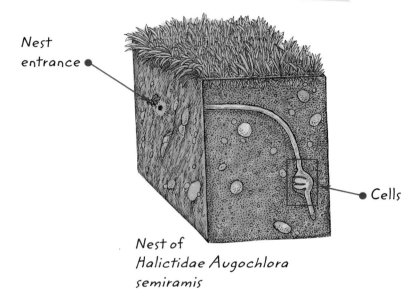

Nest entrance

Cells

Nest of
Halictidae Augochlora
semiramis

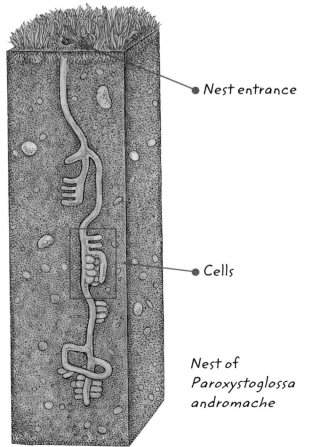

Nest entrance

Cells

Nest of
Paroxystoglossa
andromache

Who's Who

Bill keeps samples of the sweat bees he studies to help him compare different species of bees. That adds up to trays and trays of samples like the one on the right. How do scientists keep track of all these samples? They have a system.

Scientists who study insects attach two small cards to each sample they collect. On the first card, they write where and when the sample was collected. They try to be exact about the location so that they or other scientists can find the same place again later. They write the name of the insect and the name of the person who collected it on the second card.

Scientists are beginning to store the card information as bar codes, like the bar codes on packages of food in grocery stores. Scientists can then run a device over a sample's bar code and read the information on a computer screen.

Sweat bees, like this *Lassioglossum umbripenne* that Bill is holding, are very small.

Sweat bees have adapted to the environments in which they live. One species of sweat bee in Japan lives in social groups in the lowlands, where the growing season is long. But that same species has a solitary nest when it lives in the mountains, where the growing season is short. This also happens with a species in the United States. It lives in social groups in the lowlands, but it is solitary when it nests high in the Colorado Rockies. Bill hopes that the information he finds from digging up nests will help him understand more about these adaptations.

To study adaptations, Bill first needs to know about the bee society of each nest he's found. He looks at the body parts of the females under a microscope to see how many of them can lay eggs. Can all the females lay eggs or just one female? "The answer is important," Bill says. It can make a difference in the society that develops. If Bill sees

Asking Questions

Scientists who identify and give bees names are called taxonomists. To identify a bee, they start by asking yes or no questions about the way parts of the bee, such as its legs or wings, look. The answer to each question can help taxonomists identify the bee.

How does a taxonomist tell if a particular bee is is a European honeybee, a stingless bee, or a sweat bee?

1 Is the bee's back leg like the leg on the right? Is it very flat with a curvy, shiny, bald surface surrounded by branched hairs? Then it's either a European honeybee or a stingless bee.

2 Taxonomists also compare veins like the ones on these bees' wings. Are the veins at the tips of the bee's wings missing or very faint? Then it's a stingless bee.

But sometimes differences between bee species are hard or impossible to see. For example, taxonomists can see no differences between African honeybees and Africanized honeybees. Africanized honeybees are part African honeybee and part European honeybee.

that all the females can lay eggs, he has found a communal nest. If only one female can lay eggs, he has found a bee society that has one queen and many workers.

But that's not all there is to know about sweat bees. Like most scientists, Bill always has more questions. To study another sweat bee he's curious about, Bill must work in the dark.

3 Night Patrol

Henry Walter Bates was one of the world's great naturalists. A naturalist is a scientist who studies animals and plants. Bates explored the South American rain forests.

"**P**retty spectacular!" That's how Bill Wcislo describes sweat bees that fly in the dark. They are nocturnal bees. That means they're active at night.

Like day-active sweat bees, nocturnal sweat bees have many kinds of societies. Some are solitary. Others live in groups. The groups are small, with usually no more than seven females. Like day-active sweat bees, some groups have a queen that lays most of the eggs. In other groups all the females lay eggs.

Henry Walter Bates was the first person to find nocturnal sweat bees. In the mid-1800s he spent 11 years exploring the rain forests in South America. But he did not find the nests of nocturnal bees. Even 100 years later, no one knew how to find them. Bill Wcislo decided to search for the nests.

"I spent time in construction cranes that STRI has on the Atlantic and Pacific coasts of Panama," Bill says. The cranes are used to take scientists up into the treetops. "I thought that nobody had found the nocturnal sweat bees because the nests were way up in the canopy. It turns out that a lot of people, myself included, were looking in the wrong places. We were looking in tree trunks and branches that were nice and solid. And the idea of looking in the canopy was wrong, too."

Bill found out that nocturnal bees usually pick rotting, crumbly places for their nests. He was very excited to discover this. "Since then," he is happy to say, "we've marked or collected more than 250 nests. Now that I know where to look, I could easily go out and find more nests in a day than were discovered in the last 150 years."

Nocturnal sweat bees live in sticks. This is part of the reason their groups are so small. There isn't room for a large group of bees in a stick.

Just like day-active bees, nocturnal sweat bees leave their nests, gather pollen, and fly home. The home they're looking for in the dark has a "door." It is a tiny, five-millimeter (about one-quarter-inch) hole in the end of a stick.

Bill uses a special kind of binoculars called night goggles to watch the nocturnal bees. "You think this just should not be happening," he says. "Yet there they are, flying around in the dark." Nocturnal bees are so unusual that they interest other scientists who ask different kinds of questions.

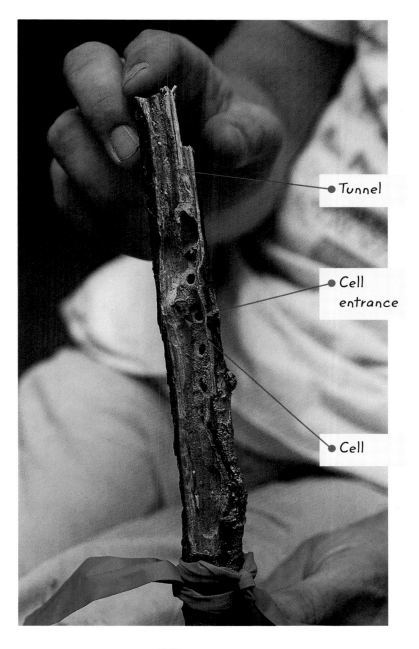

Tunnel

Cell entrance

Cell

Nocturnal bees often choose rotting, crumbly places like this stick for their nests.

Nocturnal bees are able to find their nests after every flight. Bill discovered this by using night goggles to watch bees flying in the dark.

This is a flower of the *Pseudobombax ellipticum*, or shaving brush tree. These night-blooming flowers are some of the flowers visited by nocturnal sweat bees.

Night Films

One day Bill read a paper by Eric Warrant. Eric is a scientist at the University of Lund in Sweden. He's learning how nocturnal insects see in the dark. Bill knew Eric could help him learn more about nocturnal bees. He invited Eric to visit Barro Colorado Island to study the night-flying sweat bees there.

Eric arrived with Almut Kelber, another University of Lund scientist. Almut is also interested in the behavior of nocturnal animals. She brought a special camera that lets her take pictures in the dark.

In the tropics a lot of different animals compete for food during the day. There are many kinds of pollen collectors. And there are many predators, or animals that hunt other animals for food. Imagine all the spiders, wasps, and other predators ready to pounce on a tiny bee in daylight. Bees that can look for food at night might be better off in some ways. There are fewer predators. And they can gather pollen while it's still dark, before other bees are out.

But what food can they find? Most flowers open during the day. However, all over the world, there are some flowers that bloom at night. In the tropics, especially high in the canopy, these flowers are pollinated by bats and nocturnal bees.

There may be some good reasons to look for food at night. The bees may be able to avoid enemies or collect more food. But they have to be able to make it back home again. How can they find their own little nest opening in the dark?

Many kinds of bees use scent to find their nests. Bill, Eric, and Almut wanted to know if nocturnal sweat bees mark a nest with some chemical they can smell on their return. "We swapped the sticks while a bee was away," Eric says. The bee returned and flew to the stick the researchers had put in place of her nest stick. If she used scent to find her home, she would have known this was the wrong stick.

Eric then thought the bees might use sight to find their nest. "These bees are probably learning the positions, shapes, and distances of landmarks along the way," Eric says. "To do that during the day in the forest is hard enough. But at night, with their tiny little eyes, it's mind-boggling."

And ... Action!

The scientists set up this stand and placed a bee nest on it. The camera is placed on the ground a little to the left of the stand to film the nest from underneath.

The bee nest is in this stick.

The scientists know the distance between the stripes on this box. Filming the box and the bees helps the scientists figure out the bees' flying speeds.

This stick keeps the stand from tipping over.

These disks were made sticky to keep ants from climbing up the stand and taking pollen balls, nectar, or larvae from the nest.

Almut films nocturnal bees in flight. She, Bill, and Eric study the films carefully.

Here is a picture of Almut and Eric on the first night of filming. The picture was taken using Almut's special camera.

The scientists did an experiment to see whether the bees use landmarks to find their nests. First, they chose a single nest stick and put a plastic square on it. They left it there for a while so that the bee got used to seeing it. Then, they moved the square to another nest stick nearby. The bee flew to this stick instead of to its original nest. This means it does look for landmarks.

Flight Speed

Finding the bees' speed also helps scientists understand how bees see at night. Almut films the bees leaving and returning to their nests. Eric, Bill, and Almut study the films, frame by frame, to see where the bees go and how they move. By studying the films, the scientists can learn how fast the bees fly. To do this, they have to know how far the bees fly in how much time.

Almut tells how fast the bees fly by comparing their positions in the film with the lines on a box placed near the nest. The lines are like a ruler. They are 2 centimeters (almost 1 inch) apart. Almut can tell how long it takes the bees to travel this distance because a video is really a set of pictures, or frames. Almut's video camera takes 25 frames per second. If, for example, the bees travel the distance of 15 lines, or 30 centimeters (about 1 foot), in 25 frames of Almut's film, she knows they are flying at a speed of 30 centimeters (about 1 foot) per second.

Eric says, "If you are a flying insect, you can only fly fast if you have enough light to see where you're going." This is like driving a car at night. A car's speed may depend on how well the driver can see the road. A bee's speed depends on how well it can see where it's going.

Finding Home

Different kinds of day-active bees have at least one behavior in common. Almost as soon as they're out of their nest, they turn around to face the entrance. Then, they fly in a zigzag pattern from side to side. The zigzags get bigger and bigger as the bees move away from the entrance. As they fly, they memorize landmarks near the nest to help them find it again.

Eric thinks that nocturnal bees do the same thing. "They fly away from the nest, then return from long trips of up to half an hour. So they must learn landmarks along the way, too," he says.

Almut has seen bees fly at full speed into nest holes like this one during the day. "I don't know how they do this without hitting their heads," she says.

A daytime photograph of the nest

Nest entrance

Bee

A nighttime photograph of the nest

Scientists use Almut's films to try tracing a nocturnal bee's flight as it leaves the nest. It isn't easy. The bees move very fast and the pictures aren't very clear. This is a picture made from one of Almut's films.

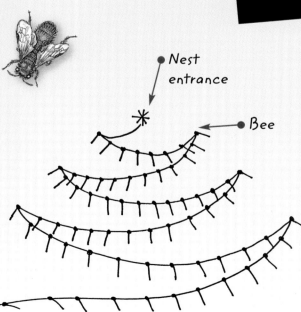

Nest entrance

Bee

The diagram at left shows the path of a day-active bee as it leaves its nest. The dots in the diagram stand for the bee's head. The lines stand for its body. The diagram shows a simple version of the flight path. Almut says, "It's really much more three-dimensional."

33

How Do Bees See?

All bees have a pair of large eyes called compound eyes. Each compound eye is made of many small lenses. The lenses collect light and form a tiny piece of an image, or picture.

Bees also have three smaller eyes arranged in a triangle between the two large eyes. The small eyes are called ocelli (pronounced oh-SELL-eye). One eye is an ocellus. Each ocellus has only one lens. These lenses don't make a very clear image.

Ocelli are used mainly to find the horizon. The horizon is the place where land and sky seem to meet. If the bee tips down as it flies, all three ocelli look at the ground. This tells the bee that it is not level, or straight. It needs to change the way it is flying. Airplane pilots use an instrument that does the same thing. It tells them when their aircraft is level with the horizon.

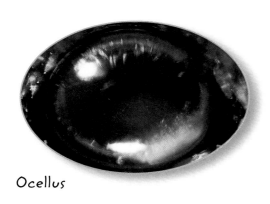

Ocellus

Ocelli

Ocelli

Compound eye

This is an artist's picture of the head of a Halictinae Lasioglossum bee. Its color is a shiny black-green.

34

Scientists are only just beginning to guess some of the things bees' ocelli do. Here you can clearly see the ocelli of these bumblebees.

To learn more about nocturnal bee ocelli, Eric removed the ocelli lenses from dead bees. Then, he looked at them under a microscope. When he did, Eric found something interesting. Nocturnal bees' ocelli are much bigger than day-active bee ocelli. But there's not much chance to see the horizon in a rain forest. So what are the bigger ocelli used for? "That's what we're here to find out," Eric says.

An ocellus has to be really big to gather light in a rain forest at night. Most of the light comes from above. So nocturnal bees may look up at that light with their ocelli. The ocelli may help them stay right-side up as they fly in the dark. These bigger ocelli are an adaptation. They help nocturnal bees fly at night.

Back in their laboratory in Sweden, Eric and Almut will look at bee ocelli again. But this time they will use an electron microscope. This powerful microscope enlarges images thousands of times. What Eric and Almut find out may help scientists discover the secret of the sweat bees' night flights.

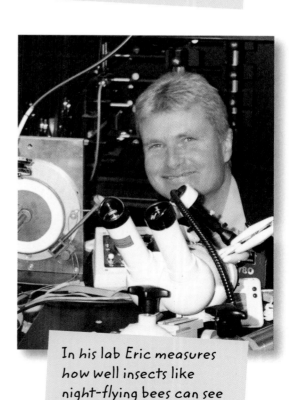

In his lab Eric measures how well insects like night-flying bees can see in flashes of dim light.

4 Fearless Defenders

African honeybees have behaviors that help them live long enough to reproduce. When the bees were brought to South America, their behaviors came with them.

What happens when a species that has adapted to one environment is suddenly introduced to a new environment? How will the new species affect other species? Will it compete with them for food? How will it affect its surroundings? Scientists had a chance to answer some of these questions when African honeybees were brought to South America.

In 1957 the only honeybees in South America were European honeybees. People kept them in groups of beehives called apiaries.

The African honeybees were shipped to a laboratory in southern Brazil. They were part of an experiment. Scientists wanted a honeybee that was better adapted to warmer temperatures.

No one is sure about what happened next. The African bees might have escaped from the laboratory. Or maybe they were let loose. Either way, they were free. They made themselves at home very quickly and soon came to be known as "killer bees."

It's no secret that killer bees have made headlines. Just the name of these insects is enough to give some people the shivers. But the stories about these bees are much worse than the facts. Bees of any kind are neither good nor bad. They just try to adapt to the environment in which they are living.

The African honeybee is no bigger than a jellybean. But it has a terrible reputation. It always seems aggressive, or ready for a fight. Scientists think that these bees are aggressive because this behavior helps them live to reproduce.

In Africa predators can easily find bee nests hanging on tree branches or on buildings. The African honey badger, for example, can quickly rip open a nest with its long claws. And people there have been taking honey and wax from bee nests for thousands of years. African honeybees adapted. They became faster and more aggressive. When many of the bees in a colony race out of a nest at once, they are fearless defenders.

European honeybees are often kept in apiaries like this one. These beekeepers are collecting honey from a beehive. The special clothing the beekeepers wear protects them from bee stings.

Bee Stings

After a honeybee stings, it dies. A wasp can sting more than once because its stinger is smooth. It slides out easily. But the stinger of a honeybee is jagged. When the honeybee tries to pull it out and fly away, its insides are ripped out along with the stinger.

If you are stung by a bee, don't try to pull the stinger out. That will only cause the bee's glands, which are attached to the stinger, to pump more poison. It's better to use the blade of a knife or your fingernail to scrape the stinger off.

Some of the stories about African bees attacking people are true. But it takes more than one of these bees to kill a person. A single sting from a bee may hurt, but it does little harm unless a person is allergic, or reacts, to the bee's poison. The sting of an African honeybee is about the same as a sting from a European honeybee. African honeybees are slightly smaller than European honeybees, so their stings may have less poison. But they attack in such huge numbers that the total poison in all of their stings can be enough to kill a horse, or a person.

So why did beekeepers want to breed African bees? African honeybees work longer and harder than some other honeybees in the tropics. That's why beekeepers admire them. African honeybees look for food at dawn. They look for food at night if there is enough moonlight. They will even fly in light rain. African honeybees travel farther to find nectar and visit more flowers on each flight than other bees. That means they have a wider choice of the best nectar and pollen. African honeybees also seem to have more resistance to diseases. These behaviors and adaptations help the bees survive.

Africanized Bees

It was easy for the African honeybees to enter the hives of less aggressive European honeybees. The African queens and drones mated with the European bees. Their offspring are more like African honeybees than European bees. They are called Africanized bees. And they are on the move.

Africanized bees, like other bees, move from place to place by swarming. Swarming is when a large number of bees move together. But the Africanized bees swarm differently from European honeybees. Most European honeybees fill their stomachs full of honey before they leave the nest. They swarm until they get hungry again. Then, they stop and usually build a new nest at that place. But Africanized honeybees can travel farther from the old nest because they stop to eat and then look for a nest farther away.

In the early 1980s, David Roubik was asked to study the first Africanized honeybees moving north into Panama and Costa Rica. He knew that people had been frightened by stories of bee attacks. They called the bees *las abejas malas,* or bad bees, and even sometimes *las abejas asesinas,* or killer bees. David wanted to see what changes had happened since the honeybees from Africa had arrived in South America.

First, David wanted to find out what plants the Africanized bees visited. But you can't easily follow bees to see the different flowers they go to. "So, I learned early on to look at the pollen," David says.

People are sometimes attacked by Africanized bees when the bees swarm.

39

To find out if the Africanized bees were visiting coffee plants (above right), David Roubik studied the food in Africanized bee cells like the ones above. When he found pollen from coffee plants in the cells, he knew that Africanized bees had visited those plants.

David says, "If you look in a cell that has a bee larva in it, you can see all the different kinds of food the larva has been given." This tells David where the bees have been going for food.

David looked at the cells of Africanized bees. He discovered that the bees were pollinating most of the coffee plants in the area he studied. Coffee plants can pollinate themselves or be pollinated by insects. David found that when Africanized bees pollinated the coffee plants, the plants produced 60 percent more beans than coffee plants that pollinated themselves. The beans on the coffee plants pollinated by Africanized bees grew faster and larger.

40

It's all because a small number of African honeybees were let go in Brazil more than 40 years ago. David wonders, "Could it be that killer bees from Africa are having a positive effect on a lot of things that people grow for food? Maybe they are."

Living Together

But what happened when the Africanized bees moved into Central America? Scientists discovered that the stingless bees and Africanized bees there visit the same types of flowers, but they make their nests in different places. Stingless bees nest in the forests. Africanized bees often live where rain forests are being cut. They like to nest in hollow, fallen trees. The species live in different parts of the rain forests, so they usually don't compete for food.

David still has more to learn about how Africanized honeybees have affected the plants, animals, and people living in South America and Central America. David says, "Having honeybees all over the place where they don't belong doesn't seem to have caused too many problems."

Aggression Test

Scientists used the comparative method to study aggression in Africanized honeybees, such as the ones pictured above. They hung a small, gently swinging ball near a bee nest. Then, they hit the nest with a stick. After 30 seconds, they slowly moved the ball.

The results? It took one type of European bees 19 seconds to sting the ball. But it was only 3 seconds before the Africanized bees attacked. The European bees stung the ball 26 times. Africanized bees stung it 64 times.

Next, the testers moved the ball away from the nest. The European bees followed it for 25 meters (about 80 feet). The Africanized bees followed for 170 meters (about 560 feet).

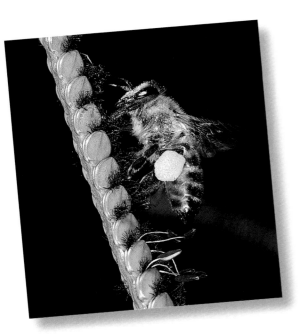

This hard-working Africanized bee forager has a full load of pollen for her nest.

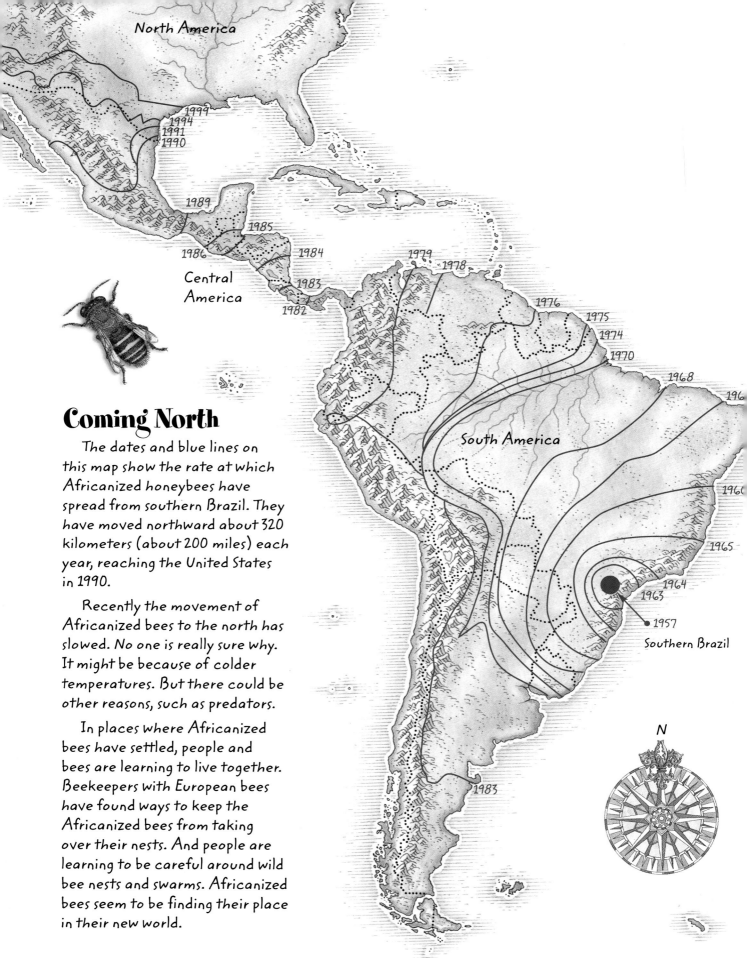

North America

1999
1994
1991
1990

1989

1985

1986

Central
America

1984

1983

1982

1979
1978

1976

1975

1974

1970

1968

196

South America

196

1965

1964
1963

• 1957

Southern Brazil

1983

N

Coming North

The dates and blue lines on this map show the rate at which Africanized honeybees have spread from southern Brazil. They have moved northward about 320 kilometers (about 200 miles) each year, reaching the United States in 1990.

Recently the movement of Africanized bees to the north has slowed. No one is really sure why. It might be because of colder temperatures. But there could be other reasons, such as predators.

In places where Africanized bees have settled, people and bees are learning to live together. Beekeepers with European bees have found ways to keep the Africanized bees from taking over their nests. And people are learning to be careful around wild bee nests and swarms. Africanized bees seem to be finding their place in their new world.

Will Africanized bees travel farther into the United States? They've already moved into Texas, Arizona, and California. But long, cold winters will probably keep them from moving much farther north. Africanized honeybees can survive short cold spells, but not months of snow.

Everything is new to the Africanized bees in North America. They are finding new flowers, new predators, new diseases, and a huge population of less aggressive honeybees. Nobody knows for sure how the bees will survive in their new environment. But scientists, like those at STRI, will be watching. As they study the secret lives of bees, scientists are always ready for surprises.

Scientists continue to study bee behavior, no matter where their studies might lead them. Here David Roubik climbs high into the forest canopy.

Glossary

African honeybee This small bee injects less poison than other bees. It attacks in greater numbers, and is far more aggressive than other honeybees.

Africanized honeybee A bee that is a cross between the European and African honeybee. It looks and behaves like the African honeybee. Also known as the "killer bee."

brood A group of young that hatched at the same time.

canopy The "ceiling" created by the leaves of treetops in the rain forest.

cells The small rooms built to hold bees' eggs.

colony A group of the same kind of plants or animals. They live together and depend on each other.

communal nest A kind of bee society in which every bee helps dig the nest, collect food, and lay eggs.

compound eye An eye made of many lenses. Each lens forms part of the image. Most insects have compound eyes.

control A copy of an experiment. The scientist can change one thing in the experiment, run both the experiment and the control, and compare the results.

drone The male bee.

electron microscope A powerful microscope that makes images thousands of times larger.

environment The conditions that surround a living thing.

European honeybee A kind of honeybee that came from Europe. It is less aggressive than African honeybees.

evolve To slowly change over many generations. Living things can develop new forms, skills, or behaviors.

forager An animal that is looking for food.

host An animal or plant in which another plant or animal finds food or shelter.

"killer bee" See Africanized honeybee.

larva A young insect.

nocturnal Active at night.

ocelli Three small eyes that form a triangle between two large eyes. The ocelli help some bees find the horizon.

parasite An animal or plant that finds shelter or food in another living thing.

pollen A powderlike material that flowers make.

pollination The first step in making seeds. During pollination, pollen is carried from a flower's stamen to its pistil.

predator An animal that hunts for its food.

queen bee A bee that lays all the eggs for a colony.

recruit A worker bee that joins foragers in the search for food.

species A group of plants or animals able to mate with one another and give birth to young that can also mate and give birth.

social Living together in a group. Only female bees are social.

society A group of plants or animals, all of the same species, that live together. All bee societies are made of female bees.

solitary Living alone.

stingless bee A type of bee that lives only in the tropics. Although a stingless bee cannot sting, it can bite.

swarm A large number of bees that move together.

sweat bee A type of bee that licks sweat.

taxonomist A scientist who classifies, or groups, living things.

worker bees The female bees that feed and care for the queen, build and guard the nest, and gather food.

Further Reading

Blau, Melinda E. *Killer Bees.* Great Unsolved Mystery Series. Austin, TX: Raintree Steck-Vaughn, 1998.

Crewe, Sabrina. *The Bee.* Life Cycles. Austin, TX: Raintree Steck-Vaughn, 1997.

Facklam, Howard and Margery Facklam. *Insects.* Invaders. New York, NY: Twenty First Century Books, 1995.

Hines, Marcia. *Killer Bees.* Mankato, MN: RiverFront Books, 1998.

Hunt, Joni Phelps, Robert Wetsel Mitchell, and Linda Mitchell. *Insects: All About Ants, Aphids, Bees, Fleas, Termites, Toebiters and a Beetle or Two.* Close Up, ed. Vicki Leon. Parsippany, NJ: Silver Burdett, 1995.

Julivert, Angels and Jose Maria Parramon. *The Fascinating World of Bees.* New York, NY: Barrons Juveniles, 1991.

Lally, Soinbhe. *A Hive for the Honeybee.* New York, NY: Arthur A. Levine Books, 1999.

Robertson, Matthew, ed. *The Big Book of Bugs!* New York, NY: Welcome Books, 1999.

Wilsdon, Christina, Annette Tison, and Talus Taylor. *Insects.* National Audubon Society First Field Guides. New York, NY: Scholastic, 1998.

Index

Acknowledgments

Turnstone Publishing Group would like to thank Bill Wcislo and James Nieh for their review of this book. The author wishes to thank Almut Kelber, James Nieh, David Roubik, Eric Warrant, and Bill Wcislo for helping her understand their research.

Photographs courtesy of Buchmann, Stephen: 6 top left, 6 bottom, 27 top; Camazine, Scott: 1, 7 top, 36, 37, 38, 40 insets, 41 top; Camazine, Scott/Photo Researchers: 39, 41 bottom; Forsberg, Lars: 32 bottom; Guerra, Marcos: 16, 27 bottom, 43; Gustafson, R./Visuals Unlimited: 30 bottom; Knight, Chris: 2, 26, 29, 30 top; Kelber, Almut: 31, 32 top, 33; McDaniel, Stephen: 35 top; The Natural History Museum: 28; Nieh, James: 10, 11, 12, 13, 14, 15, 17, 18, 19; Oxford Scientific Films/Fogden, Michael: 3; Oxford Scientific Films/Morris, S.R.: 40 main image; Oxford Scientific Films/David Thompson: 7 bottom; Vetter, Rick: 7 middle; Warrant, Eric: 6 top right, 34, 35 bottom; Wcislo, Bill: 20, 21, 22 top and bottom, 23, 24 top and bottom.

Illustrations on pages 2, 3, 4, 5, 6–7, 9, 19, 20, 23, 25, 27, 28, 29, 31, 33, 34, 36, 42, and 43 are by Patricia Wynne. The small bees were drawn from specimens in the collection of the American Museum of Natural History, New York. The following books were also used as illustration references: Shoichi F. Sakagami and Charles D. Michener, *The Nest Architecture of the Sweat Bees* (Lawrence, KS: The University of Kansas Press, 1962); Stephen L. Buchmann, "Buzz Pollination in Angiosperms," in *Handbook of Experimental Pollination Biology*, edited by C. Eugene Jones and R. John Little (New York, NY: Scientific and Academic Editions, 1983); Charles D. Michener, Ronald J. McGinley, and Bryan N. Danforth, *The Bee Genera of North and Central America* (Washington, D.C.: Smithsonian Institution Press, 1994).

Maps on pages 8 and 42 are by Dave Stevenson.

Diagram on page 33 is by Almut Kelber.